TECHNOLOGY AT WORK

AT THE
BUILDING SITE

Richard Spilsbury

www.raintreepublishers.co.uk
Visit our website to find out more information about Raintree books.

To order:
☎ Phone 44 (0) 1865 888112
🖹 Send a fax to 44 (0) 1865 314091
🖥 Visit the Raintree bookshop at www.raintreepublishers.co.uk to browse our catalogue and order online.

Raintree is an imprint of Capstone Global Library Limited, a company incorporated in England and Wales having its registered office at 7 Pilgrim Street, London, EC4V 6LB - Registered company number: 6695582

"Raintree" is a registered trademark of Pearson Education Limited, under licence to Capstone Global Library Limited

Text © Capstone Global Library Limited 2009
First published in paperback in 2010

Edited by Louise Galpine and Rachel Howells
Designed by Richard Parker and Tinstar Design Ltd
Original illustrations© Pearson Education Ltd
Illustrations by Darren Lingard
Picture Research by Hannah Taylor and Catherine Bevan
Originated by Modern Age
Printed and bound in China by CTPS

13-digit ISBN 978 1 4062 0983 9(hardback)
13 12 11 10 09
10 9 8 7 6 5 4 3 2 1

13-digit ISBN 978 1 4062 0990 7(paperback)
14 13 12 11 10
10 9 8 7 6 5 4 3 2 1

British Library Cataloguing in Publication Data
Spilsbury, Richard,
    At the building site. - (Technology at work)
    681.7'6
A full catalogue record for this book is available from the British Library.

Acknowledgements
The publishers would like to thank the following for permission to reproduce photographs: ©A1 Pix Ltd p. 4; ©Alamy pp. **9** (WoodyStock/Alfred Schauhuber), **17** (Picpics), **23** (Michael Doolittle), **26** (Dennis MacDonald); ©Construction Photography pp. **6** (Rae Cooper), **13** (Adrian Greeman), **15, 21-22**; ©Corbis/ H. David Seawell p. **29 bottom**; ©Cumulus p. **29**; ©David Haggerton Photography 2008 p. **20**; ©Jupiter Images/ liquidlibrary p. **29 mid**; ©Pearson Education Ltd pp. **28 top** (Ian Wedgewood), **28 bottom** (Gareth Boden); ©Photodisc p. **29 top**; ©Photographers Direct p. **20**; ©Photolibrary/ Brand X Pictures p. **11**; ©QA p. **19**; ©Science and Society Picture Library p. **27**; ©Superstock/ Pixtal p. **7**.

Cover photograph of new building under construction , reproduced with permission of ©Corbis/ Joel W. Rogers.

We would like to thank Ian Graham for his invaluable help in the preparation of this book.

Every effort has been made to contact copyright holders of any material reproduced in this book. Any omissions will be rectified in subsequent printings if notice is given to the publishers.

CONTENTS

Some words are printed in bold, **like this**. You can find out what they mean by looking in the glossary.

BUILDING WORK

Building sites are places where people make structures. Sites can be big or small. It depends on the size and number of structures. The site of a large supermarket is bigger than a site of one small house.

Making work easier

Builders use many different **machines** to help with their work. A machine is a device that makes a **force** bigger. Forces are pushes or pulls. For example, hitting a nail with a hammer pushes a nail easily into wood. You could not push the nail in with your finger because the force needed would be too great. Workers use machines so jobs take less **effort**.

What machines are workers on this building site using to help them dig, carry, and build?

On a slope

On a building site you sometimes see workers moving heavy vehicles or materials in **wheelbarrows** up slopes. These slopes are called **ramps**. Ramps are one of the simplest machines. Workers use less force to carry a weight up a long slope than to lift it straight up.

The idea of using ramps for moving materials has been used since Ancient Egyptian times.

AT WORK

PYRAMID BUILDER

In Ancient Egypt, builders used sloping ramps made from earth to lift huge blocks of stone so they could build the pyramids!

KNOCK DOWN!

Some building sites are on empty land. Sometimes builders have to **demolish**, or knock down, old buildings before they can build something new.

Smashing forces

Workers use heavy tools to demolish. The weight adds extra **force** to a smashing blow. Sledgehammers are long hammers with heavy heads. Workers swing the hammer against hard materials.

A breaking ball swings from a chain to smash walls down.

Breaking force

A **wedge** is a simple **machine**. It is shaped like two **ramps** back to back. When you hit a wedge, it changes the downward force into sideways forces.
A chisel is a metal bar that has a wedge-shaped end. You use it to break open hard **concrete** or stone. The power of a chisel tip is greater than a hammer head because its force is centred on a much smaller area. Pickaxes and jackhammers are tools with chisel ends.

Air pushed into the jackhammer

Chisel splits open the ground

AT WORK

AIR FORCE

The force of a jackhammer is produced by air. A pump blows air hard against a steel rod inside the jackhammer so it knocks fast against the chisel end. A jackhammer chisel can strike concrete 1,500 times each minute!

CLEARING THE SITE

Workers use powerful **machines** called bulldozers to clear broken bricks, metal, and other rubble from building sites. The bulldozer's strong blade scrapes along the ground, pushing rubble out of the way.

Get a grip!

Bulldozers are very heavy. Instead of wheels, they have caterpillar tracks. These help bulldozers move over muddy ground without sinking.

Caterpillar tracks are made of plates of thick steel linked together in a band. The area of track supporting the bulldozer on the mud is much larger than individual wheels. This means that the weight of the vehicle is spread over a wider area. That is why the bulldozer does not sink into the mud.

Ridges on the bulldozer's caterpillar tracks grip the mud to stop it slipping as it works.

1. The track is moved by a sprocket wheel turned by the engine.
2. The blade scrapes rubble along.
3. Bulldozer tracks move at different speeds to change direction. For example, when the right-hand track goes faster, it forces the bulldozer to turn left.

AT WORK

SUPERDOZER

The superdozer is the biggest bulldozer in the world. It has a blade 7 m (23 ft) across and it can push rubble that weighs as much as several school buses!

DIGGING MACHINE

Workers make the building site flat by digging and shifting soil. They do some digging with shovels but mostly use a **machine** digger to save **effort**. A digger has a strong arm made of giant steel parts. The arm moves a bucket at its end and the bucket does the digging.

Liquid power

The digger operator makes the arm move using **rams**. These are the parts on the digger shaped rather like bicycle pumps. A ram is made up of a cylinder (tube) with a plunger that can slide in and out of it. The digger's engine pumps oil through long, thin pipes into the cylinder. The oil pushes the plunger powerfully.

Ram

The small force acting on the oil through the narrow pipe creates a big force acting on the oil in the wider cylinder.

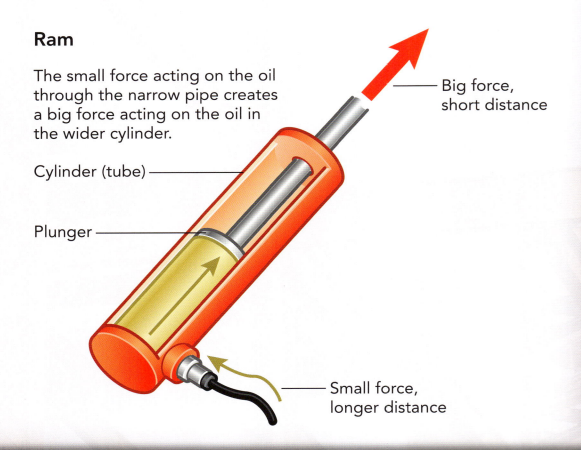

Cylinder (tube)

Plunger

Big force, short distance

Small force, longer distance

1. Drivers operate a digger from a glass cab next to the arm. From here they can see what they are digging.

2. Rams control the movement of different parts of the arm.

3. Teeth on the bucket are **wedge**-shaped to help it cut into the hard soil.

Buildings are very heavy and must be able to stay standing in strong winds. They need a firm base called **foundations** to stop them sinking into the ground or falling down!

IN THE FUTURE

Tall buildings over 1.6 kilometres (one mile) high will be built to fit more people into overcrowded cities. Imagine how strong their foundations will have to be!

Digging deep

Building workers use **machines** to help them make foundations. A piledriver is like an enormous hammer. It knocks steel beams and **concrete** posts down through soil until they rest on solid rock deep underground. Sometimes workers use a foundation **drill**. The drill spins and its sharp **wedge** cuts holes in rock or hard soil. Workers fix foundations to concrete in the holes to form a stable base for a building.

AT WORK

DEEP DRILLS

A drill is a tool with a sharp point and cutting edges. As you turn it quickly again and again it makes holes in hard materials. The kind of drills used in oil wells can go down as far as 8 kilometres (5 miles) deep!

Here you can see a piledriver driving a concrete post, or pile, deep into the ground.

BUILDING MATERIALS

People build using many materials. They may make floors from **concrete**, walls from bricks, and roofs from wood, tiles, and steel beams. Most materials are transported on lorries from the place they are made to the construction site.

Hard stuff

Concrete is the most common building material in the world. Concrete is useful because it starts off as a thick liquid that then sets hard and strong. Therefore concrete can be made in any shape, from blocks to flat sheets.

People make liquid concrete by mixing together cement powder, gravel or sand, and water. It takes a lot of **effort** to mix these ingredients using a shovel, so workers use a cement mixer. Some cement mixers make enough concrete to fill a **wheelbarrow**, but others are so big they are fitted on the back of special trucks.

AT WORK

INSIDE A CONCRETE MIXER

The drum of a concrete mixer spins around. This sloshes the concrete ingredients against a **screw**-shaped blade in the centre. The blade mixes up the ingredients properly. The movement helps keep the mixture liquid until it is time to pour out the concrete.

Change direction! A concrete mixer spins one direction to mix concrete and the other way to pour it out.

WEIGHT-LIFTING

Building materials are heavy to lift. Workers use different **machines** to move heavy weights around the building site. These include cranes, **wheelbarrows**, and **pulleys**.

Lifting wheels

A wheel with a grooved rim and a rope looped around it is one of the simplest lifting machines. This is called a pulley. Pulling down on one side of the pulley lifts up a **load** on the other side. The pulley wheel changes the direction of the **force** needed to lift a weight.

Several pulleys used together make lifting even easier. It takes half the **effort** to lift a load when a rope is wrapped around two pulleys. So workers can lift twice the load with the same strength of pull used on one pulley. The only problem is that workers have to pull the rope twice as far to lift the load!

Pull! Workers use their body weight to help pull down on a pulley rope to lift something up. Using a system of pulleys, construction workers can lift huge loads that they would never be able to lift alone.

MIGHTY LIFTER

The mightiest lifting **machine** at the building site is a tower crane. It can lift many tonnes high into the air.

In the balance

When a tower crane lifts a heavy **load** from one end of its boom (long bar), it looks as if it might topple over. It does not because a heavy **counterweight** hangs from the other end.

The boom is a type of **lever**. A lever is a simple machine that rests on a point called the **fulcrum**. A lever balances when two similar sized loads hang from either end, rather like a seesaw. It also balances when a heavier load hangs from one end, as long as this weight is nearer to the fulcrum.

1. The boom is supported on the tower. The point where they meet is a fulcrum.

2. Boom.

3. **Pulley**. A motor in the crane pulls on a cable that passes through the pulley to lift weights.

4. Counterweight. This giant **concrete** block balances loads lifted on the other end.

5. Strong cables from the very top of the tower help to support the boom and counterweight.

AT WORK

SELF-BUILT

Tower cranes can build themselves section by section! Giant rams raise the crane by 6 metres (20 feet). Then a new section of tower is put in the gap.

FRAMEWORKS

Buildings need **frameworks** to support them. Some have brick walls on their **foundations** to support the building above. Skyscrapers have reinforced **concrete** frameworks to support them. Walls and windows hang off the framework once it is built.

These builders are guiding steel beams into place to form the framework of a high building.

AT WORK

REINFORCEMENTS

Reinforced concrete has steel mesh or bars put into it before the concrete sets hard. This makes the concrete extra strong. A reinforced concrete framework can support 500 times its weight.

Joining up

Most frameworks are made up of separate parts joined together. Workers sometimes use nuts and bolts (see below) to hold the parts in position. They sometimes **weld**, or melt, metal parts together using a very hot flame. The metal sticks together once the melted metal cools.

Goggles protect workers' eyes when welding. Welding makes heat and a very bright light.

Nuts and bolts

Bolts have a short, wide head and a long, narrow spiral thread. The thread is shaped a bit like a **screw**. Twisting a nut onto the thread pushes it closer to the bolt head. This squeezes together parts held by the nut and bolt.

Cutting tool

Cutting tools are called saws. A saw has many sharp triangles called teeth. The edges of the teeth are sharp and **wedge**-shaped to push open cuts. Workers use their arm muscles to move hand saws back and forward. They can cut using less **effort** by using electric-powered saws.

After they have completed the **framework**, workers add walls, ceilings, water pipes, electric cables, and floors inside. They cut different materials into different shapes to finish off buildings. For example, they cut out pieces of wood to make frames for stairs.

Spinning teeth! A circular saw has a disc with teeth around the edge to cut tough concrete blocks.

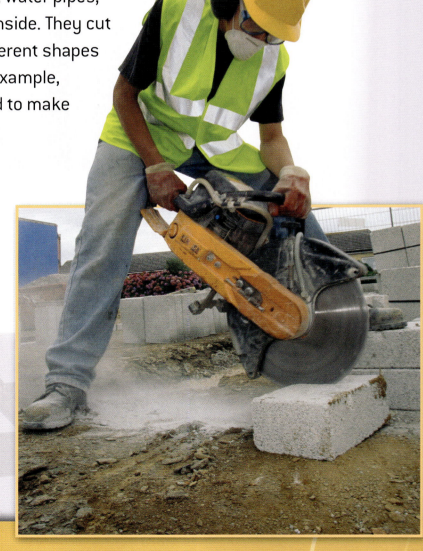

Plasterers work more quickly using stilts than when they have to go up and down a step ladder.

Spring balance

Plasterers make walls and ceilings smooth. They use metal blades to scrape a paste called plaster over surfaces. Plasterers have to work fast before plaster sets hard. Some wear **stilts** strapped to their legs to plaster ceilings. **Springs** inside the stilts help keep the stilts upright as plasterers walk around doing their work.

FAST WORK!

Many of the wooden pieces inside a building are fixed together with **screws** and nails. Turning a screwdriver makes the spiral **ramp** around the edge of a screw cut into wood or other materials. A nail is like a sharp **wedge**. It splits open a hole when it is knocked in with a hammer.

It takes time to pick up a nail or screw and then operate a hammer or screwdriver. On a building site workers often use **machines** to fix more quickly. They use electric **drills** and nail guns with belts of screws and nails attached. These machines launch nails very quickly, placing them in the material in just a fraction of a second. The next screw or nail is automatically ready to use as soon as the last one is put in.

AT WORK

SPEED NAILING
A nail gun can hammer in between 20 and 30 nails every minute!

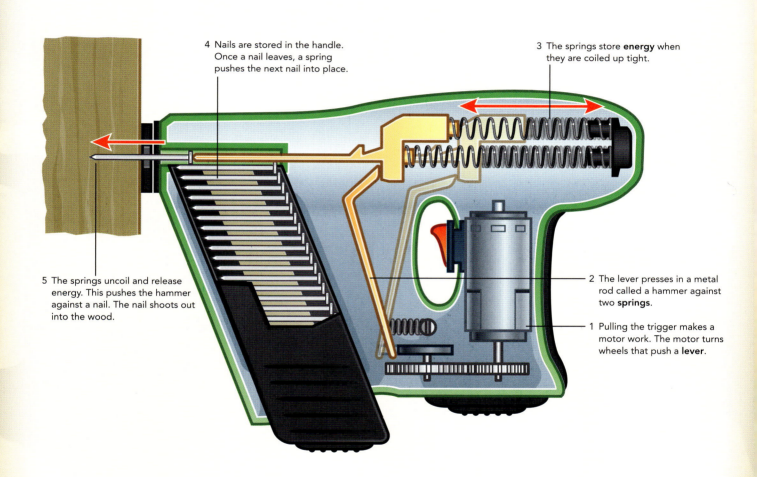

4 Nails are stored in the handle. Once a nail leaves, a spring pushes the next nail into place.

3 The springs store **energy** when they are coiled up tight.

5 The springs uncoil and release energy. This pushes the hammer against a nail. The nail shoots out into the wood.

2 The lever presses in a metal rod called a hammer against two **springs**.

1 Pulling the trigger makes a motor work. The motor turns wheels that push a **lever**.

Whoosh! Every nail shoots fast from a nail gun like this to fix materials together.

ROADS AND TUNNELS

Workers on a construction site use special **machines** to build roads. Without roads people would not be able to get to and from their new homes!

Road layers

Workers build roads using layers of different materials such as gravel and a sticky material called asphalt. Workers tip the materials from a tipper lorry into a paving machine. The paving machine moves slowly forward and spreads out the material to the right thickness. Then workers drive rollers with wide, heavy steel and concrete wheels over the road. This rolls the top layer to make a hard and smooth surface for people to drive on.

Teams of workers drive different machines to lay roads.

Boring but interesting! Giant tunnel borers like this can cut tunnels many metres wide.

Going underground

Tunnel borers are special machines that cut tunnels through solid rock. At the front a tunnel borer has an enormous rotating cutter. It also has a **conveyor belt** to remove the cut pieces. The belt is a moving band of wire mesh behind the cutters. It catches the falling rock and carries it away.

AT WORK

SWISS TUNNELLING

In 2007 a new tunnel was built below the Swiss Alps that is 57 kilometres (35 miles) long. It is the world's longest land tunnel.

BUILDING MACHINES

The wide variety of tools and equipment on a building site all work using simple **machines**. These are **ramps** and **wedges**, **screws**, **levers**, hammers, and **rams**. Some use several machines together to do their work.

RAMPS AND WEDGES

A wedge is a simple triangular shaped machine that can be used to **force** things apart. Wedges make up the blade of saws and **drills**, and the ends of chisels, jackhammers, and pickaxes. A ramp is a slope or ledge that goes from one level to another, higher level.

chisel   pickaxe

nail   jackhammer

saw

SCREWS

Screws are simple machines that change turning or rotating movements into up, down, or side-to-side movements. A screw has a straight part that has a tiny ramp winding around the outside of it. Screws do work in cement mixers, drills, and nuts and bolts.

screw   nut and bolt

cement mixer

drill

LEVERS

Most levers are a rod or bar that rests on a point called a **fulcrum**. When you push down on the long end of a lever, it increases the force at the short end. The increase in power is used in crowbars. Some levers have an axle instead of a fulcrum. Twisting the wide end of a screwdriver with a small force turns the narrow end with a bigger force.

screwdriver   tower crane   crowbar

HAMMERS

A hammer is a machine that creates large pushing forces. The forces are usually made by moving a heavy metal end with a handle or a chain. They can also be made using spring power.

breaking ball   nail gun   sledgehammer

RAMS

Rams create pushing and pulling forces using liquid such as oil or water pressing inside enclosed spaces. Rams move in or out to shift the arms of diggers and bulldozers, and to raise the heights of tower cranes. They are a bit like levers because they turn a small push over a long distance into a powerful push over a short distance.

digger   bulldozer   tower crane   **pulley**

GLOSSARY

concrete building material made from sand, gravel, cement, and water. Concrete walls are strong and hard.

conveyor belt moving belt that transports objects. A conveyor belt has a continuous loop of material that keeps turning.

counterweight weight that balances another weight. On a crane the counterweight balances the load.

demolish to break up or knock down. Sledgehammers are used to demolish some old buildings.

drill tool with a sharp point and spiral, cutting edges. A drill turns a screw-shaped head in order to cut holes.

effort use of energy. It takes effort to push a wheelbarrow or use a hammer.

force pushing or pulling action. We use a pushing force to make wheelbarrows work.

foundations base of a building. The foundations are what make a building stable.

framework structure that supports something. A skeleton is the framework that holds your body up.

fulcrum support or point on which a lever rests

lever simple machine that helps us lift loads. A seesaw is a kind of lever.

load weight that has to be moved or lifted

machine device that helps us do work. Hammers are machines that help us bang nails into wood.

pulley wheel with grooved rim that rope passes through. Pulleys help us lift and shift loads.

ram device that uses the push of liquid to do work. In a digger, a ram makes the arm move up and down.

ramp a sloping surface. You might find a ramp at a skateboard park!

screw simple machine that is like a ramp or slope wrapped around a bar. This screw thread is what makes nuts and bolts and drills work.

spring coil of metal. When you squash a spring, it creates a force that is released when the spring goes back to its original shape.

stilt pole that you stand on. Stilts help people walk high above the ground.

wedge triangular shaped machine that can be used to split logs and stones. We also use a door wedge to keep a door open.

weld join metal parts by melting them together

wheelbarrow cart for carrying loads. A wheelbarrow has one wheel at the front and handles at the back you lift and push.

FIND OUT MORE

Books

Construction Zone, Cheryl Willis Hudson (Candlewick Press, 2006)

Levers (Very Useful Machines), Chris Oxlade (Heinemann Library, 2004)

On the Building Site (Machines at Work), Ian Graham (QED Publishing, 2006)

On the Building Site (Machines Rule), Steve Parker (Franklin Watts, 2008)

Pulleys (Very Useful Machines), Chris Oxlade (Heinemann Library, 2004)

Pushes and Pulls (Construction Forces), Patty Whitehouse (Rourke Publishing, 2007)

Ramps and Wedges (Very Useful Machines), Chris Oxlade (Heinemann Library, 2004)

Screws (Very Useful Machines), Chris Oxlade (Heinemann Library, 2004)

Websites

www.edheads.org/activities/simple-machines
You can learn more about simple machines such as levers, and play games.

www.mikids.com/Smachines.htm
Find out more about simple machines such as wedges.

www.omsi.edu/visit/physics/engineerit/structures.cfm
Have a go at building your own structures using machines like pulleys and cranes.

INDEX